THE ALNWICK
GARDEN

Everyone should spend a day in...

...The Garden

Contents

1 The Grand Cascade

2 The Ornamental Garden

3 The Rose Garden
Supported by David Austin Roses

4 The Woodland Walk

5 The Treehouse
Supported by the Northern Rock Foundation

6 The Poison Garden
Supported by the Claire Bell Fund

7 The Serpent Garden
Supported by the William Leech Charity
and the Claire Bell Fund

8 The Bamboo Labyrinth
Supported by the Barbour Trust and
the Claire Bell Fund

9 The Water Tower

10 The Pavilion
and Visitor Centre

11 The Garden for the Senses
still to come

12 The Spiral Garden
still to come

13 The Quiet Garden
still to come

14 The Cherry Orchard,
Grotto and Pond
still to come

15 The Central Garden
still to come

16 The Pavilion Garden
still to come

17 The Treehouse Play Area
still to come

To the town
3 minute walk

To the castle
3 minute walk

A living landscape

The Alnwick Garden is a charity committed to changing the cultural landscape. As well as standing for contemporary gardening excellence, The Garden provides real benefits to people through play, learning, the arts, healthy activity, addressing disability and the economic renaissance of a rural community.

During your visit you will see evidence of this commitment, firstly in the quality training that has been given to our staff who have a range of backgrounds and needs. In The Treehouse and The Pavilion and Visitor Centre, you will enjoy good seasonal produce that has been locally sourced and have the chance to buy local goods. In The Garden you will see children playing and older people taking part in stimulating activities, and everyone can enjoy the diversity of experience offered by the arts and education programmes.

This is a living landscape of ideas and opportunities. By supporting The Alnwick Garden Trust, you will help this dynamic and inspiring project complete the vision of a world-class garden to be enjoyed for generations to come. You will also provide the resources needed by The Trust for its charitable work, delivering benefits to people and their communities in the following areas:

Promoting skills and lifelong learning

Skills and lifelong learning enrich the lives of individuals, communities and our wider society.

- provides on-the-job training for young people and long-term unemployed
- offers programmes in science and the arts to schools and teachers
- provides crafts and arts activities such as poetry and gardening

Engaging people in a broad range of the arts

By bringing the arts into The Garden, we are enabling thousands of people, who would not usually be interested in visiting traditional arts venues, to experience different forms of the arts. Examples of the arts in The Garden are:

- Architecture and sculpture
- Music, including live jazz and world music in The Treehouse
- Street theatre and storytelling in The Garden

Encouraging people to think positively about disability

The Garden believes in taking proactive action to ensure a truly enjoyable experience for disabled staff and visitors. It does this by:

• working with agencies such as Scope and The British Legion to provide job opportunities for people with disabilities/learning difficulties
• hosting arts and performances involving disabled artists
• encouraging children of different abilities to play together

Widening opportunities for young people to play

The Alnwick Garden aims to enable children to enjoy outdoor play that gives them as much choice, control and freedom as possible in a safe environment. Examples of play activities are:

• annual play week for children and families
• training for play professionals
• being the play garden for the Alnwick Children's Centre

Encouraging healthy activity for all and active ageing

To promote health, happiness and wellbeing, The Alnwick Garden will be running a series of programmes including:

• activities designed by and for older people to reduce isolation
• drug awareness programmes
• healthy lives programmes

Promoting economic renaissance

The Alnwick Garden has already (and will continue to) help the economy of the region by:

• providing jobs
• encouraging local product development
• helping to make the region an all-year destination
• welcoming visitors to Northumberland

The Design Team

The Duchess of Northumberland is The Alnwick Garden's creative visionary and leads the design team. The Duchess is a trustee of The Alnwick Garden Trust, the charity that owns and operates The Garden, and volunteers her time. She is a keen gardener and particularly interested in gardens as public spaces.

The Duchess selected the world-renowned Belgian landscape designer Jacques Wirtz and his son Peter to create The Garden. Their Master Plan is a fascinating combination of quiet and busy spaces, with the gentle and introspective Rose Garden feeling far removed from the children playing in the water jets of the Grand Cascade. The design is supported by strong green structures, an important element of the Wirtz design and visible in the beech hedges, clipped hornbeams and yew.

These structures repeat throughout and hold the diverse themes and unique features together, and ensure that The Garden provides interest all year round. In winter, the structure is evident and visitors are able to see the bones of The Garden, while in summer it provides the backdrop for exuberant flower displays.

Leading British architect Sir Michael Hopkins was chosen to design The Pavilion and Visitor Centre.

Jacques Wirtz

Born 1924, Antwerp, Belgium.
Studied Landscape Architecture and Horticulture at the Tuinbouwschool Vilvoorde. Founder of Wirtz Landscape Architecture and Wirtz International, contracting and design companies. Design of gardens and parks throughout Europe and worldwide.

Peter Wirtz

Born 1963, Schoten. Belgium.
Studied Landscape Architecture at the Tuinbouwschool, Melle. Since 1986 has worked as a Landscape Architect for Wirtz International and Wirtz Landscape Architecture.

Sir Michael Hopkins

Senior Partner of Michael Hopkins and Partners, founded in 1976. Awarded a CBE and knighted for Services to Architecture, and won the RIBA Gold Medal for Architecture in 1994.

An artist's aerial view of
The Garden proposals, showing
the myriad of water
courses, features, hedges,
plantations and
buildings

Giovanni Antonio
1697–1768

A detail from Canaletto's painting
of Alnwick Castle in 1752

The History of The Garden Site

one of the finest public gardens in over two years

Triple arch into the future Ornamental Garden
July 1997

The site on which The Alnwick Garden is built has had a colourful history, with previous gardens built here designed by the leading contemporary designers of their day.

12

The History of The Garden site

The Triple arch
July 1997

Remains of the last
conservatory

View to the south from the
site of the last conservatory -
now a piece of history

The 1850 pond - used by the
Percy family as an ice-skating
rink in past winters

Hugh Smithson
Earl and 1st Duke
1750-1786

Hugh Percy
2nd Duke
1786-1817

Hugh Percy
3rd Duke
1817-1847

Algernon Percy
4th Duke
1847-1865

The first garden was laid down in 1750 by the 1st Duke of Northumberland who employed locally born Capability Brown, the most celebrated gardener of the day, to landscape the parkland adjoining the castle grounds.

Alnwick Castle gardens then underwent a century of development. Hothouses were built for raising pineapples and produce was sent to Paris for the 3rd Duke when he was special ambassador there in 1825. This Duke, who was a plant collector, brought plants and seeds from all over the world to be reared at Alnwick. He built a large conservatory in the gardens which were opened to the public one day a week. For her part the 3rd Duchess transformed the site into a garden of flowers.

The reputation of the gardens attracted important visitors from abroad, and in the 1800s the head gardener of Tsar Alexander 1st of Russia visited and subsequently 'head-hunted' Alnwick's head gardener, who left for Russia.

About 200 years old,
*The Fox Urn was
bought by the 10th Duke
with winnings from
a horse race and was
donated to The Alnwick
Garden in 2000.*

15

The gardens were at their most complete in the mid-19th century when the 4th Duke re-created stunning new gardens in the Italian Renaissance style reflecting his work in The Alnwick Castle at the time.

The 4th Duke purchased two pairs of 16th century Venetian wrought-iron gates from Italy. These have been restored and are re-hung in their original positions in The Alnwick Garden, at the main entrance and at the entrance to the Ornamental Garden.

At the end of the 19th century the gardens were at their grandest with yew hedges in topiary, a double avenue of limes, acres of flower garden, five grape houses, five pine houses and a conservatory.

Past Designers

The most important garden designers and architects of their day worked at Alnwick. In addition to Capability Brown, Decimus Burton (mostly noted for The Palm House and Temperate House at Kew Gardens) also influenced the gardens at Alnwick, although these designs are long gone.

The Development of The Alnwick Garden

The contemporary Alnwick Garden is being developed using the historic footprint of previous gardens.

Historical Features

As well as its own network of engineering and water pipes, the present Grand Cascade is adjacent to the remains of vast underground tunnels that provided hot air for earlier greenhouses. The heat was provided by large underground coal-fired furnaces.

Other historical features still visible in The Alnwick Garden are the two large earth banks that run down either side of the Grand Cascade. These were first constructed in the garden of the 1850s and became the starting point for The Alnwick Garden. The main axis of the Grand Cascade runs down to The Pavilion and Visitor Centre, which was the site of a previous pavilion in the 1860s.

A historic garden decoration can also be found. It is an early 18th century lead sculpture of a fox sitting atop a fruit-filled urn decorated with masks depicting the four seasons and supported by monkeys.

Two World Wars and the austerity of the 20th Century saw the garden site fall into disrepair. During the Second World War, the site provided food when it was turned over for the Government's 'Dig for Victory' campaign, a 1942 scheme that called for every man and woman in Britain to keep an allotment. The site was closed as a working garden in 1950 and used as a tree nursery before The Alnwick Garden project began in March 1996. Since then, visitors to The Alnwick Garden have been able to watch history being made once again, as the site has become a magical landscape full of ideas, opportunities and fun.

The Grand Cascade

7,260 gallons of water

July 1997

April 2001

July 2001

June 2003

The Grand Cascade runs down the main north south axis of the site and forms the centrepiece for the entire garden. Constructed in a series of 21 weirs, 7,260 gallons of water per minute tumble down it at peak flow.

Made of Darney Stone from West Woodburn in Northumberland, the Grand Cascade is split into two apparent sections. Water falls down the first 18 weirs, disappearing into four large bell mouth openings, to reappear at the other side of the terrace. In total there are over 323 metres of weirs in the Cascade.

The water displays within the Grand Cascade are switched on at 10am daily and change sequence every half-hour throughout the day, with four sequences in total.

During the sequences, three large central jets reach a height of six metres, with 40 smaller jets sending water four metres into the air. 80 side jets form parabolas of water to the centre of the Grand Cascade and four jumping jets issue from the four bell mouths, firing streams of water over the terrace into the lower basin. The climax of the display is an eruption of fountains forming a mass of water, which, at its peak, reaches a height of six metres.

The sequences are computer-controlled by state of the art equipment in the pump room below the Grand Cascade.

The Grand Cascade

850 hornbeam pergola

The Grand Cascade has been designed to be as environmentally friendly as possible. As such, 250,000 gallons of water are stored underground at any given time, and are filtered and recycled. The Grand Cascade re-circulates its water up and down a vertical drop of 10 metres.

In the event of heavy rain, overflow water is discharged directly into the nearby River Aln, without fear of contamination.

At the base of the main watercourse, the visitor is surrounded by the noise and splashing of water. From here, crescent-shaped stairs lead up to the intermediate level. From this belvedere, it is possible to continue up on either side of the Grand Cascade or turn onto pathways under hornbeam pergolas.

The 850 hornbeams have been specially imported from Van Den Berk's nurseries in Holland; they were brought to The Garden as ten year old standards and are being trained to a metal frame

support. Designed with 'windows' facing out onto it, the visitor will be uncertain once the trees mature, where the walk starts and ends.

Key facts

• 250,000 gallons of water are stored underground at any given time, and are filtered and recycled. The water is re-circulated up and down a vertical drop of 10 metres

• 149,000 block paving stones have been used around the Grand Cascade and its pergolas – it would take you all day to count them.

• 850 hornbeams line the Grand Cascade.

• In total there are over 323 metres of weirs in the Grand Cascade.

At the top of the hill,
down which the Grand Cascade
is built, lies a smaller walled
garden accessible through three
inter-linked stone arches.

22

The Ornamental Garden

The Ornamental Garden

a masterpiece of

planting

July 1997

April 2001

July 2001

June 2003

Three 500-year-old wrought iron Venetian gates span the arched entrance to the Ornamental Garden.

Wirtz International designed this element of the Ornamental Garden to extend visual interest. By using a play of light and shade, grey and green foliage, flowers and fruit in the intricate planting pattern, Wirtz not only created a masterpiece of planting on the ground, but also created a beautiful lacework in the air using pleached crab apples.

This rectangular, walled plot lies between the main area of The Garden and the edge of the town of Alnwick, screened by a belt of trees.

The Ornamental Garden

Key facts:

- There are 16,500 plants in the Ornamental Garden.
- The bricks which make up the walls were originally brought to England as ships ballast.
- The Venetian gates at the entrance to the Ornamental Garden were bought as antiques and date back 500 years.

At the centre of the Ornamental Garden is a pool from which a series of rills flow. Pergolas surrounding the central pool are covered in ramblers and vines.

The rills lead to yew-enclosed 'secret' gardens, accessible from two sides, one with a red colour theme, and one with yellow.

The basic square design is repeated many times throughout The Garden, sometimes divided diagonally by hedges and sometimes surrounded by pleached crab apples, which create 'rooms' of blossom in the air in springtime.

Around the central pergola, boxwood-edged beds house a collection of bedding roses surrounded by delphiniums. Further from the pergola, cut flower species alternate with annuals and bulbs alongside small fruit varieties. In the more irregular exterior spaces, Cornus mas hedges enclose collections of Hydrangea paniculata cultivars.

At the perimeter of the Ornamental Garden lies a wide herbaceous border with rose-covered arbours in the corners.

The planting is designed to flower at different times of the year creating swathes of colour with perfume and mass.

The entire planting scheme is designed to draw the eye of the visitor through The Garden and extend visual interest, delight and intrigue. Attractively designed 'oversized' Douglas fir benches, which complement the scale of The Garden, are placed throughout the Ornamental Garden and two dovecotes attract peaceful winged visitors.

At the right of the fore-garden lies the Rose Garden.
This part of The Garden has its own pergola-lined
walkway and an array of specimen roses.

The Rose Garden

The Rose Garden

a beautiful rich

pink rose

July 1997

November 2000

May 2001

June 2003

The Alnwick Rose

To coincide with the creation of The Alnwick Garden, a new English rose was launched by David Austin at the 2001 Chelsea Flower Show. The Shropshire-based nursery has produced a beautiful rich pink rose, called the Alnwick Rose, with cup-shaped buds gradually opening into a deeply cupped flower, later developing into a broad, full-petalled, shallow cup of a soft pink which is paler at the outer edges.

The new rose has a delicious Old Rose fragrance with a hint of raspberries, round bushy growth and it blooms continually from early summer to the onset of the frost. It has plenty of green foliage that complements 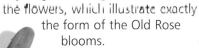 the flowers, which illustrate exactly the form of the Old Rose blooms.

The Rose Garden

3,000 bushes and

climbers

The Alnwick Rose joins other English, Old, Shrub and climbing roses in the Rose Garden.

Everyone involved with The Alnwick Garden has a favourite rose; our garden volunteers who help with the dead heading of the roses in peak season will tell you the best roses to use for rose petal sorbet, the Duchess may favour a rose because of its understated beauty, our Head Gardener, because of the continual splendour of a particular bloom. Whatever your passion for roses we are sure that you will not be disappointed by the fragrance and beauty offered the Rose Garden.

Pergola lined pathways lead through the Rose Garden where the visitor will witness a tumbling mass of fragrant blooms each with a name which conjures up romantic images. Look for Jude the Obscure, Gertrude Jekyll and of course, the Alnwick Rose.

Key facts:

- A total of 3,000 rose bushes and climbers create a massive splash of colour.

- When providing roses to The Alnwick Garden, David Austin Roses gave us a very strict regime of care to follow. Our gardeners regularly spray and feed the roses according to this regime.

- The feed is one of our Head Gardener's special secrets but he will hint that seaweed is involved.

experience centuries
of change

34

The Woodland Walk

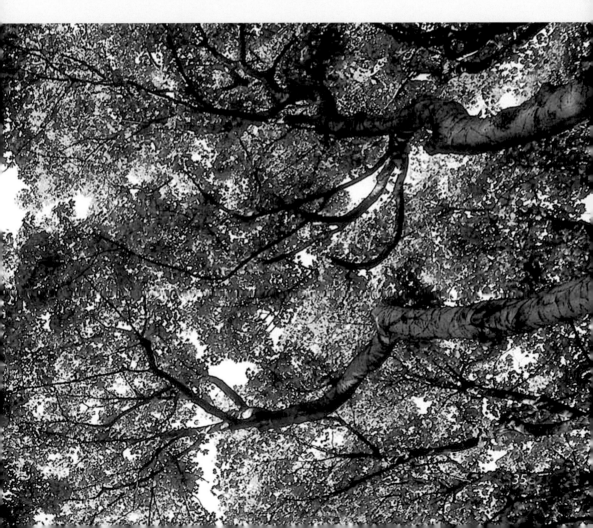

The Woodland Walk

Mature trees, many of which have seen centuries of change, line the naturally undulating pathway to the River Aln. Spring buds of green promise a seasonal change, in summer a canopy of leaves provides a dappled light effect which is magical to the eye. In autumn the colours arrest the senses and in winter the magnificent structure of the trees attract all manor of feathered friends to make the Woodland Walk a nature watchers paradise.

Its here that you will enjoy the panoramic views of the River Aln and the sweeping vistas towards Alnwick Castle landscaped by Capability Brown.

The Woodland Walk provides a contrast to the more formal gardens. Spring flowers and wild garlic carpet the ground along the walk while the visitor can enjoy the views of Alnwick Castle and Capability Brown landscape from the Duchess's viewpoint

one of the world's
largest wooden tree
houses

The Treehouse

Opened in January 2005, the construction of one of the world's largest wooden tree houses was an opportunity to make The Alnwick Garden an unrivalled experience for everyone. A place to learn, play and relax, The Treehouse is a 6,000 sq ft complex of turret topped cottages linked by suspended walkways, high in the trees outside the walls of the main garden.

The Treehouse project has been as exciting as it is innovative.

Access is via a ramp and so The Treehouse, its rope bridges and walkways in the sky are accessible to everyone, including wheelchair users.

The Treehouse has been built using natural materials from sustainable resources including Canadian Cedar, Scandinavian Redwood and English and Scots pine, and the quirky design is so at home in its environment that it appears as if The Treehouse has been there for many years. Visitors can experience, at close quarters, the world of trees - the filtering sun through a leaf canopy and swaying, creaking branches over, under and around them.

The Treehouse includes two resource rooms, the Nest and the Roost, which is equipped with the latest technology to host The Garden's learning programmes. There's also the Treehouse Shop, full of inspired gifts and educational toys for children, a timber-decked veranda and at the heart of The Treehouse is a wonderful place to eat.

Future plans for The Treehouse

The Alnwick Garden Trust are currently fundraising for the next phase of The Treehouse's development; an exciting tree-based adventure play area which will be accessible to children of all ages and abilities.

Although the play area is still in the planning stages with the final design yet to be confirmed, we do know that it will set a new standard in the quality of play facilities. Designed to be 'safely dangerous', the play area will incorporate a maze of rope bridges, platforms and aerial walkways, with wheelchair access. At various levels there will be activities that take place across the natural small ravine, and a designated area for the under 5s and for the severely disabled. Much of this will be a covered space, and The Treehouse area will then accommodate over 1000 people.

The Serpent Garden

In the Serpent Garden, eight water sculptures nestle in the coils of a topiary serpent, each showing a different aspect of water and how it can be made to look and move. Created by William Pye, one of the world's leading water sculptors, these mirror-polished artworks use science and interactivity to fascinating effect.

The serpent is formed from holly, while the sculptures are each within large beds of yew.

The simplicity of William Pye's designs combines with the complexity of the movement of water.

lashes, trickles, flows,
waves and reflects

41

The Serpent Garden

The sculptures are:

Coanda

This sculpture shows the Coanda effect which makes water cling to the underside of smooth overhanging surfaces, appearing to defy gravity. The Coanda effect was discovered by Henri Coanda, a famous aeronautical engineer who went on to develop a flying saucer. He studied sculpture with Rodin and engineering with Alexandre Eiffel.

Meniscus

This sculpture shows a meniscus, which is the convex surface of the water at the top of the sculpture. A meniscus is created because the water molecules on the surface stick together to make an invisible skin, this skin is called surface tension. Some insects, like water striders, can walk on water because the surface tension is strong enough to hold their weight.

Vortex

This sculpture shows a vortex, which is the air core at the centre. Water creates a vortex as the forces of water pressure, air pressure and gravity make it move downwards in a spiral. There are many vortices in nature, like tornadoes and the black holes of the universe.

Reflection

This sculpture shows a reflection. Reflection both extends and compresses space and depths become unpredictable. Here it transforms a hemisphere to a sphere. The mirror-like hemisphere reflects the colours around it, the green of the hornbeams and the blues, whites and greys of the sky.

Canyon

This sculpture shows water creating rollwave patterning as the thin film flows down its smooth surfaces. Surface tension pulls the water into these rhythmical wave patterns, surface tension happens when the water molecules on the surface stick to each other. A canyon is a narrow, steep-sided valley, like the space in the middle of this sculpture.

Canyon

Coanda

Meniscus

Torricelli

This sculpture shows water under hydrostatic pressure, which fascinated the 17th century Italian physicist, philosopher and mathematican Evangelista Torricelli. This is the pressure that comes from the head or the distance between the surface of the water and a point below, regardless of the volume of water.

A pool on high ground overlooking the Serpent Garden overflows to fill up the sculpture below through underground pipework.

The water rises in the transparent tubes until it is level with the surface of the nearby pool, representing the head of water that has been reached.

A pneumatically powered valve below the ground opens to release the hydrostatically charged water into a circular manifold that feeds ninety jets that leap vertically up and then gradually subside in unison with the dropping levels visible in the transparent tubes.

When these jets have all but died the valve closes, allowing the system to fill up again and the cycle to continue.

Starburst

This sculpture shows water jetted upwards onto a glass surface, moving outwards to create a thin sheet of water. This thin sheet of water is unstable, and surface tension pinches it to form droplets that fill and stretch until they reluctantly drop away into the abyss below.

Waterglass

This sculpture shows a single curtain in the form of a transparent, clear, unbroken membrane of falling water wrapping around a circular enclosure that can be entered and experienced from within, the outer views seen through the thin film of water. When there is no wind the film can be as clear as glass. The flutter effect at the foot of the water curtain is a cyclic phenomenon caused by a difference in pressure on each side of the water which causes it to suck to and fro.

The Poison Garden

Dangerous plants, from belladonna to tobacco, can be found in the Poison Garden, a dramatic garden full of mystery and intrigue. The Poison Garden is a place to hear ancient plant lore and learn about the dangers of plants with the potential to kill, from specially trained Poison Garden Wardens.

 The use of poison dates back as far as spiritual and mythical beliefs have been recorded. Our ancestors knew about the power of plants, not only which parts of plants were poisonous, but also what quantities to use to kill, to cure, to drug or to relieve pain. Most children today know that if stung by a nettle you must find a dock leaf, but what happened to all the other plant knowledge we once had at our fingertips?

The locked wrought iron gates remind visitors of the danger within the Poison Garden, and once visitors emerge from the gloomy, ivy-covered tunnels, the flame-shaped beds lick at their feet. Some plants are so dangerous they are kept behind bars.

Caroline Holmes, garden historian, author, broadcaster and designer, working as a consultant for the Poison Garden, selected the planting to fit with the Wirtz designed garden. Caroline says, "It's meant to be something of a secret place containing wild plants to poison the mind and body".

With Home Office approval, drugs such as cannabis and magic mushrooms are grown in the Poison Garden, and programmes are being developed in consultation with the Education Department's Drug Action Team.

If you would like to know more about the plants in the Poison Garden, look out for the fascinating book available in our shops for £5. The book is also available by mail order please call 01665 511350.

The Bamboo Labyrinth

Planted with a new Chinese variety of bamboo 'Fargesia' rufa on waist-high banks, the Bamboo Labyrinth is very different to the time-honoured labyrinth.

Set in a windy corner of The Garden, the Bamboo Labyrinth rustles around the mysterious twisting paths that merge and divide like a fast-flowing stream. The paths are scattered with bronze leaves that look as if they have been blown down from the bamboo.

This walk-through, entertaining feature was designed by Adrian Fisher, one of the world's leading maze-makers. He is known for maze design with distinctive patterns and exquisite puzzles. His work includes a world record breaking 'maize maze' in USA, Blenheim Palace hedgemaze, the RNIB maze for the blind and Jersey Water Maze.

The Visitor Centre and Pavilion

The Pavilion and Visitor Centre are stunning contemporary buildings designed by the British Hopkins Architects led by the Duchess. They integrate beautifully into the landscape and bring an extra dimension to The Alnwick Garden experience, providing a theatrical entrance.

The Pavilion and Visitor Centre has been described by Wirtz International, The Garden's designers, as the stage from which the theatre of The Garden can be presented. When coming through The Pavilion's arched entrance into the Walled Garden, The Garden opens up before the visitor and the performance begins.

The bespoke design based on the concept of merging the indoor and outdoor spaces and using predominantly transparent materials, ensures that the visitor continues to experience The Garden while inside the buildings. Throughout, there is an exposed structural frame comprising steel and timber columns and a timber barrel-vaulted roof with lightweight pillows. The Visitor Centre surrounds a courtyard, and terraces extend from The Pavilion into The Garden landscape. On one side, the terrace features planting of fastigiated beech that will grow to form a tall tower of trees creating a focal point in the topiary structure of the lower garden.

The design makes a poetic reference to glasshouses that stood on the site in a previous garden many years ago, while using the latest technology and environmentally-advanced services.

Features include ground source heat pumps that utilise energy from geothermal bore holes to provide space heating and cooling, together with a similar system for general water heating. Five metres below The Visitor Centre is the Rockstore, this provides a thermal 'battery' so that surplus heat generated by visitors and sunlight can be recycled to warm or cool the spaces later. Rainwater and spent cooling water is harvested for toilet flushing, and the design allows predominantly natural lighting and ventilation. Timber throughout has come from sustainable resources.

The buildings feature spaces to eat, drink, shop and relax, and are a home for many of The Garden's programmes. There are also two resource rooms, and a regional information centre.

Still To Come

Vision to reality

The first two phases of the Master Plan are now in place, and The Alnwick Garden Trust are fundraising for Phase Three. Future developments at The Garden will include:

The Treehouse Play Area

An exciting tree-based adventure play area, The Treehouse Play Area will be accessible to children of all ages and abilities. Designed to be 'safely dangerous', the play area will incorporate a maze of rope bridges, platforms and aerial walkways, with wheelchair access.

The Garden for the Senses

A garden where your senses are used to their fullest, an eclectic mix of plants have been selected for the Garden for the Senses. They will stimulate smell and touch, and water will provide interesting sounds. Experiencing this garden with a wheelchair and blindfold will help children to understand the importance of the senses.

The Spiral Garden

The Spiral Garden will create a high point to climb to through a colonnade created with pleached hornbeams. At the base, marbles of water will be spurted for children to catch and smash.

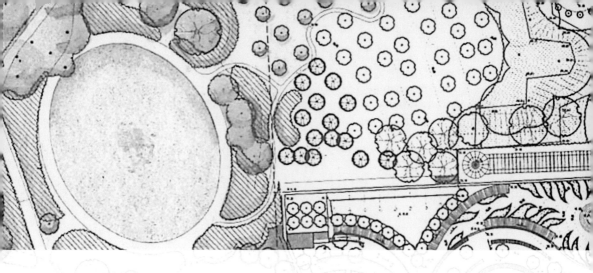

The Quiet Garden

A place to relax and read a book, the Quiet Garden will feature a large shallow pool. Paddle or have a picnic on tables and chairs sited in the water.

The Cherry Orchard, Grotto and Pond

In the Cherry Orchard, open paths will lead to a picturesque landscape with more than 300 specimen Tai Haku cherry trees. The Grotto will use salvaged stone to build a ruined folly with a waterfall fed by the natural spring that feeds the Pond. The re-landscaped Pond will feature an ice sculpture with spectacular lighting and possibly an ice rink.

Enjoyment by day and by night

Finally, The Garden will be extensively lit, emphasising the waters of the Grand Cascade and other displays. Visitors will then be able to enjoy The Garden at all times of the day and evening and in all seasons.

Arts in The Garden
are eclectic, quirky and fun.

The Garden gives visitors the opportunity to experience and engage with a broad range of the arts. Working in partnership with local, national and international artists, The Garden is home to events and activities for all the family that range from music and street theatre to storytelling, puppetry, aerial performances and creative workshops. Much of the programme is free after paying admission to The Garden.

The Garden hosts special arts events from Springfest, a festival of dance, A Fairies Tail involving aerial performances to shows involving light, contemporary cabaret or Jazz.

The Treehouse has become a regular venue for live music, to accompany the delicious menus served. As well as jazz from some of the North East's finest jazz musicians, there's also the chance to hear a range of performers and musical styles from folk and blues to classical and world musics.

For details of the arts programme, see www.alnwickgarden.com or call 01665 511350 to join our mailing list.

Learning in The Garden

Learning in The Garden is inspiring, informal and for everyone.

The Garden is home to educational experiences that stir the imagination, stimulate curiosity and foster a love of learning skills. From Play Week to Science Week and the Big Draw, there's always something interesting to try or fun to do.

For adults, there's an ever-growing range of courses and classes. With garden or plant specialists to yoga courses in beautiful settings, there really is something for everyone.

For details of the learning programme, see www.alnwickgarden.com or call 01665 511350 to join our mailing list.

There's also a range of resources available for schools visiting The Garden, a natural resource for many learning activities.

Eating and drinking, shopping and holding events

The Garden is a lovely place to relax over something to eat or drink or to take time choosing gifts and treats, and a stunning venue for an event or celebration. Choose from the quirky interiors of The Treehouse, or The Pavilion and Visitor Centre's light and contemporary spaces.

All surplus revenue is channeled back into the project, so when eating and drinking, shopping or holding an event, you are helping bring the landscape to life.

Eating and drinking

For a quick coffee, a light lunch or a very special dinner, eating in The Garden is a delicious experience.

You'll always find good, seasonal produce that has been locally-sourced and prepared in imaginative ways. We believe in providing choices, including healthy menu options, children's menus and table or self service.

The unique dining experience offered by The Treehouse is nothing if not unusual, the roaring log fire, fascinating craftsmanship and dimmed lighting create an other-worldly environment.

Morning teas and coffees with pastries, breads and sandwiches, delicious lunches and afternoon tea are served every day to your table. There are seasonal specials throughout the year.

The Treehouse is open for dinner on Thursday, Friday and Saturday evenings from 6pm, with last orders taken at 9.30pm and a choice of set and à la carte menus available. The Treehouse may open for dinner at other selected times during the year, call or see www.alnwickgarden.com to find out. On selected evenings The Treehouse also features live music, call 01665 511852 to make a reservation.

In The Visitor Centre, the Courtyard Coffee Shop serves great coffee, drinks and snacks.

The Pavilion features a self-service space that overlooks The Garden's landscape, tables and chairs spill onto the terraces. Choose from an ever-changing selection of hot dishes, soups, salads, sandwiches, cakes and drinks that include smoothies, wines and beers.

Shopping

Shopping at The Alnwick Garden is a real pleasure, whether you're looking for

something to take home to remind you of your visit, high quality gardening goods and plants, an interesting gift for someone or just an enjoyable browse.

The Treehouse Shop, amongst the branches and on the decking, is inspired by nature and is stocked with educational toys for children, bugs and beasts, books and homeware.

There are two shops in The Visitor Centre, the Garden Shop and the Gift Shop. As well as lovely Northumbrian produce, the Garden Shop features gardening goods and plants including beautiful roses from David Austin Roses. The Gift Shop sells original gifts, accessories, home and tableware, books and souvenirs, including postcards.

Tickets are not required in The Visitor Centre, and so visitors can shop and visit the Courtyard Coffee Shop at no charge.

Some great things are available by mail order; interesting books such as

'The Making of The Alnwick Garden' by Ian August, and The Alnwick Garden exclusive range of gifts and garden accessories.

Holding events

The Alnwick Garden, with beautiful gardens and stunning contemporary architecture, is a world-class venue for inspiring events.

The Pavilion and Visitor Centre uses a blend of wood, steel and mellow stone to provide multi-function spaces for exhibitions, conferences, business events, weddings and celebrations.

The atmospheric and intimate spaces within The Treehouse are perfect for business events, parties and dinners, for up to 90 people.

To plan something special, call our events team on 01665 511350.

Be a part of The Alnwick Garden

You may have already supported The Garden by visiting and including a donation in your ticket purchase. You can support The Alnwick Garden Trust further by becoming a Friend, a Supporter and a Volunteer.

Become a Friend of The Garden

Give perennial support by becoming a Friend, and you can become an important part of The Alnwick Garden community. Enjoy The Garden throughout the year and through the seasons as it matures, and watch future developments take place as The Garden moves from vision to reality.

An eclectic programme of events runs throughout the year, many of them at no additional charge once you have purchased a Friends subscription. As a Friend you can bring up to four children with you each time you visit, so as well as enjoying the breadth of the programme yourself, you can open up a world of creativity and activity to the children you know.

As a Friend you'll receive:

Quick and easy unlimited access to The Garden during normal opening hours

Quarterly Friends newsletters

Exclusive Friends opportunities and invitations

To become a Friend, please call 01665 511350.

Become a Supporter of The Garden

Help The Garden grow by becoming a Supporter, providing some of the 20,000 plants and trees still needed. You can play your part in bringing this exciting vision to life and shaping history. Whether your gift buys roses, clematis, hedging or trees, there will be a part of The Garden that you have helped to create.

You can begin to support The Garden with just £10, choose from the following donations:

£10 £25 £50 £250 £750 £2000+

All Supporters will be kept up to date with Garden news and receive a thank you pack appropriate to the level of support given.

There are other ways you can help us, including sponsoring a motorised wheelchair or a plot in the Ornamental Garden, or buying a bench or a tree for the Cherry Orchard.

To support The Garden, please call **01665 511358**.

Become a Volunteer at The Alnwick Garden

If you like to be hands-on, becoming a Volunteer is an extremely rewarding way to support The Alnwick Garden and become directly involved in the project.

From guides to gardeners and from retail staff to administration staff, we are lucky to have a team of Volunteers who invest their valuable time in working for The Garden. There is always much to be done, and help is always appreciated.

There are many interesting opportunities, and working for The Garden can be extremely flexible. To find out more about volunteering and talk about how you would like to help,

call 01665 511350.

HRH Prince Charles and the Duchess of Northumberland at the opening of The Alnwick Garden.

HRH the Prince of Wales

Alnwick Castle and its great park lie at the heart of some of Britain's finest scenery, and the huge castle garden forms an integral part of the landscape.

Created over three generations from the middle of the 18th century, the garden in it's prime reflected the personal commitment and vision of successive Dukes of Northumberland and the professional skill of gardeners of the highest reputation, such as Lancelot Brown and Decimus Burton. This was to become one of Britain's most admired gardens, enjoying a century of magnificence and splendour which was brought to an end by war and severe financial restraint some fifty years ago.

In seeking to recapture the lost world of this great garden, and sharing it with others, the present Duchess of Northumberland is taking up once more the innovative ideas so brilliantly demonstrated in previous generations. The proposed designs will not simply recreate the past, but also provide for a variety of educational and botanical uses needed in the century to come.

The project is a bold and ambitious one which I am delighted to support. The garden will be a true work of art for everyone to enjoy, and a statement both of gratitude to the past and hope for the future. I wish the project every possible success.

Charles

2001

A Year In The Garden

January

Begin the year with a New Year's Day walk in The Garden, the architectural attraction is arguably strongest at this time. Evergreen Viburnum tinus (white flowers) and deciduous Viburnum 'Dawn' (pink, highly scented), started blooming in October. Tall standards of the winter cherry Prunus subhirtella 'Autumnalis' are similarly appealing at this time. In the Ornamental Garden, Crab apple fruits persist at eye level 'Evereste' and above 'Red Sentinel'. The biggest surprise is when the Hellebores 'Early Purple''Wester Flisk' and foetidus start blooming in defiance of the weather.

February

Bulbs follow in numbers. Tens of thousands have been planted and the effect is stunning. A veritable carpet of chionodoxa, scilla, daffodil, et al illuminates the Water Tower walk up to the Ornamental Garden. Three reliable shrubs are flowering too. Chimonanthus praecox (yellow, scented), Daphne mezereum (red/purple, scented) and Cornus mas (yellow) are a welcome sight.

March

The chorus of bulbs has by now reached a crescendo with the addition of the colonising Crocus 'tommasinianus' (purple/blue). A group of camellias which include 'Donation' and 'Daintiness' are gorgeous but 'Cornish Snow' (evergreen with white flowers) is the tops. Look out for Pulmonovia 'Munstead Blue', 'Sissinghurst White' and saccharata, whose flowers are at first pink then change to sky blue.

April

Peripheral borders in the Ornamental Garden are really awakening now with three favourites; Epimedium x rubrum (crimson/yellow), dog-toothed violets (in many colours) and the pendulous Dicentra formosa offering great cheer.

May

Climbers dominate in the nicest possible way! Varieties of Clematis montana cover walls and pergolas with mounds of flowers, whilst a totally different evergreen Clematis armandii

offers clusters of highly-scented white blooms. Early roses emerge on the south wall of the Rose Garden. Meanwhile, up through the triple arches, green and variegated forms of the herbaceous forget-me-not (Brunnera macrophylla) are flowering.

June

In the Ornamental Garden find the shrubby mock orange (philadelphus), Jerusalem sage (phlomis) and valerian (centranthus). And don't miss the tall (8') yellow scabiosa (Cephalaria gigantea). Highlight of the year for many is the first and best flush of roses, which arrives around Midsummers Day. Many forms are represented, from the earliest dating circa 1300, to David Austin's creation (English Rose), the first of which was raised 30 years ago. The summer programme of activities begins this month, with fun and interesting workshops and activities and live performances of music and street theatre in The Garden's unique landscapes and settings.

July

Walk through the arches and be greeted by giants. Delphiniums over 10 feet tall

('Spindrift') cannot be ignored. Eye catching soft fruits are there to be found and tasted! There are red and yellow strawberries and gooseberries, in beds punctuated by glorious standard roses. A full range of currants (red, white and black) is fruiting alongside the curious blackcurrant-gooseberry hybrid called a jostaberry.

August

Herbaceous geraniums are a magnet for various species of bumble bee, whose flight paths also take in the distinctive flowers of Rudbeckia 'Goldsturm' (yellow) and Scabiosa 'Clive Greaves' (violet blue). In the Poison Garden, admire the flowering display of Nicotiana sylvestris (tobacco plant) and Hycoyamus niger (henbane) from a safe distance.

September

At least five species of butterfly continue to flourish on the herbaceous perennials. Most notable are the crimson/pink coneflower (Echinacea purpurea) for peacocks and painted ladies, and Joe Pye weed (Eupatorium purpureum) for red admirals.

Clumps of Lythrum salicaria offer rose red blooms in a border whilst Clematis orientalis 'Bill McKenzie' (yellow with black stamens) dazzles on a wall. In the Poison Garden, Atropa belladonna (deadly nightshade) fruits have turned black and are at their most lethal.

October

Clematis and roses continue to entertain. Clematis 'Duchess of Albany' (light and dark pink) and 'flammula' (white/cream flowers) accompany the dark red hips of rugosa roses. Autumn fruiting raspberries in red and yellow appeal to birds and visitors alike and everywhere there is glorious leaf colour. Hot spots for this are the hornbeams that line the Grand Cascade, deep reds and purples on various prunus and the climbing Vitis vinifera purpurea. In the Bamboo Labyrinth, Fargesia rufa (hardy bamboo) sways so in the autumn wind that the whole area appears to be flowing. This is a hardy plant that can stand up to 20°c and flower in winter. Look for the Cercidiphyllum japonicum (Katsura tree) between The Treehouse and disabled car park. Pick up and rub some of the fallen smoky pink/yellow leaves to release the scent of burnt sugar. Experience Halloween in The Garden, a time of fun, spooky events and workshops.

November

The pink, double flowers of Dendranthema rubellum 'Anjas Bouquet' shine through shortening days. Yellow fruit clusters on Malus 'Butterball' are outstanding while curious-shaped fruits on the medlar tree (Mespilus Germanica) are just beginning to rot and are ready for use.

December

The tall winter cherry Prunus autumnalis 'Rosea' and a bush specimen of 'The Bride' are blooming merrily. Emergence of the winter hellebores provides a reminder that we've just gone full circle. Christmas in The Garden is a special time, to see Santa, shop for lovely gifts and decorations and to celebrate with family and friends over delicious seasonal food and drink. Covered in pretty white lights and with carol singers on the decking, The Treehouse is truly magical at this time of year.